This book belongs

to

the awesome :

....

....

RUM
RUM

RUM

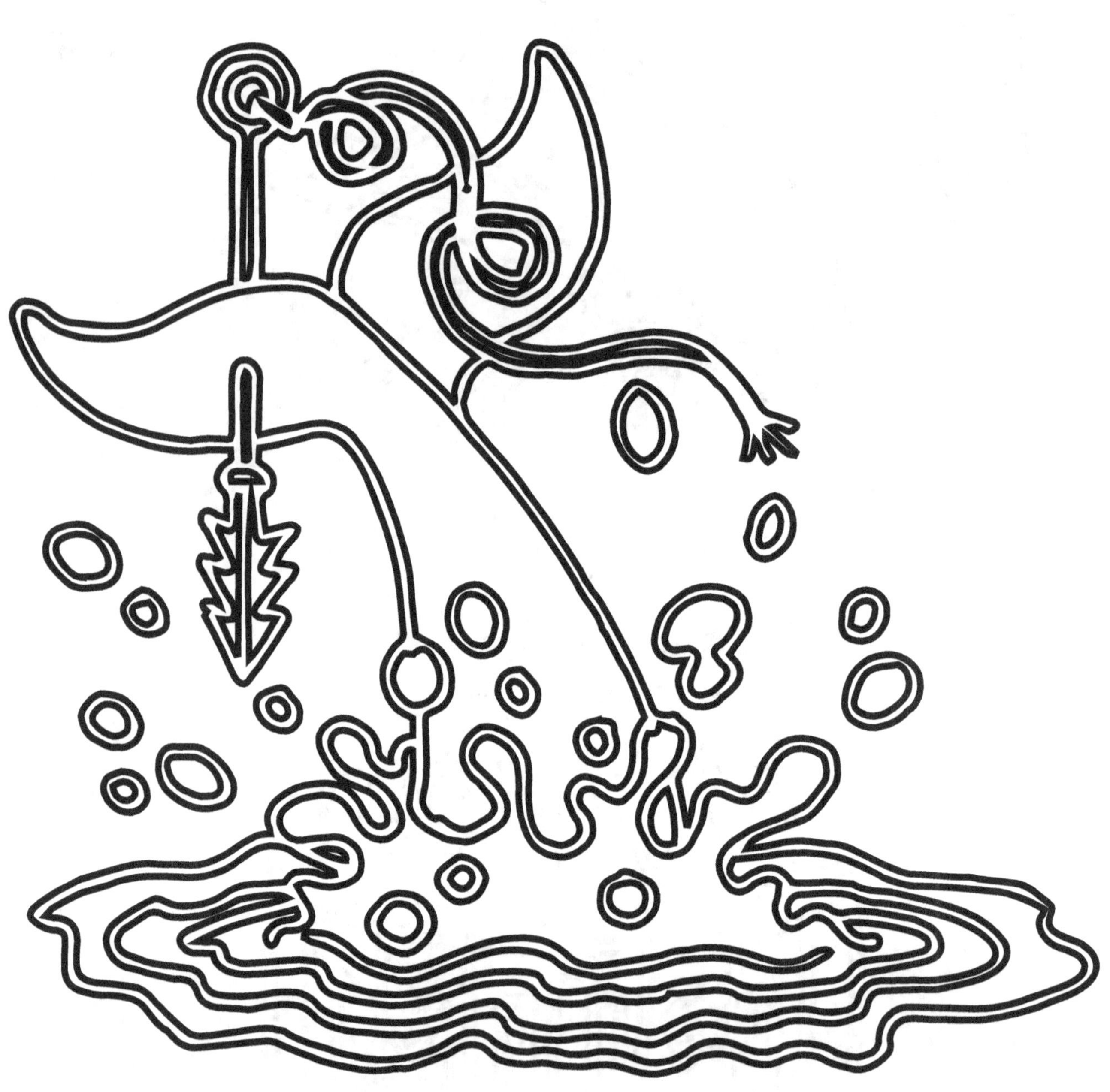

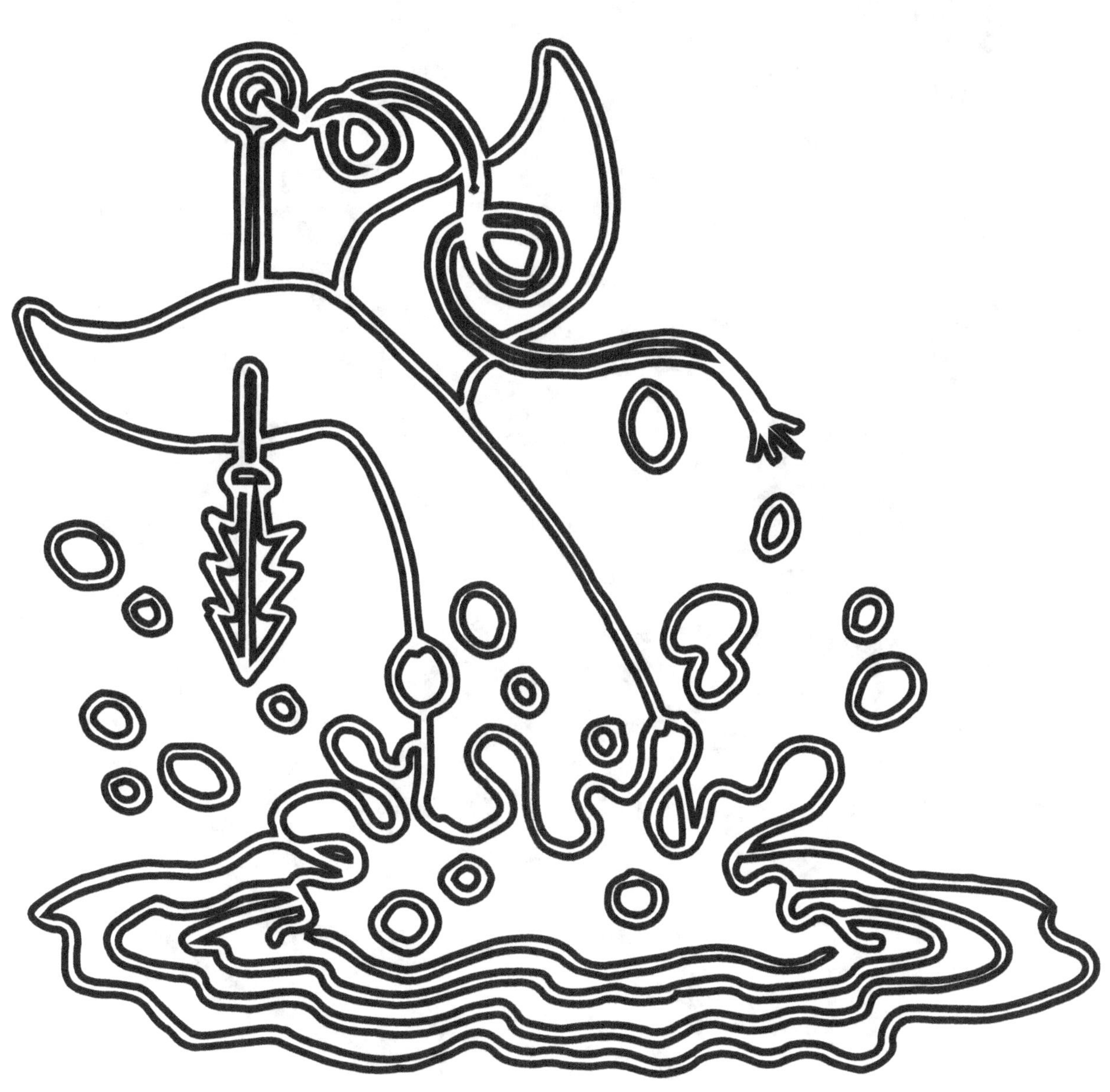

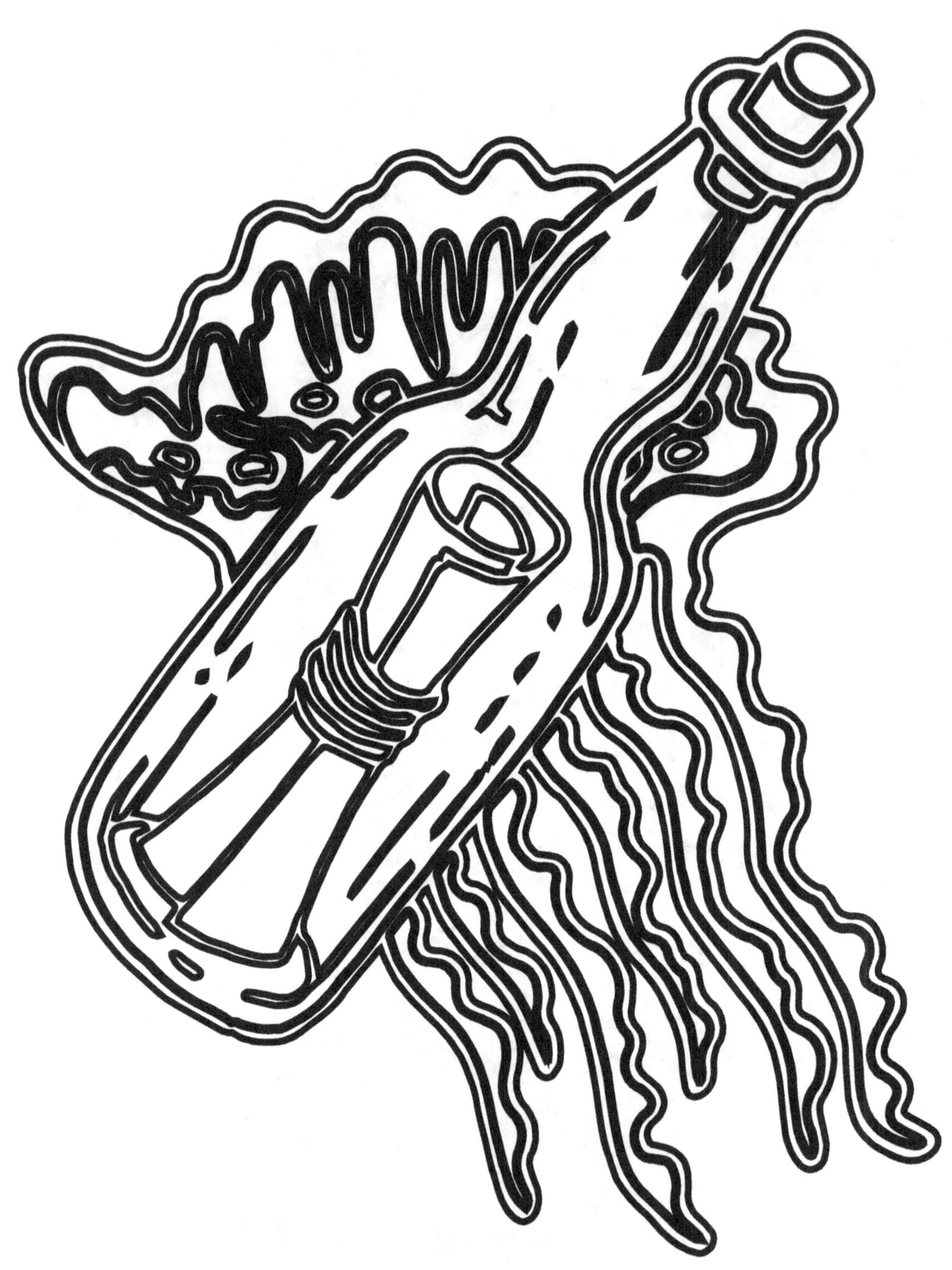

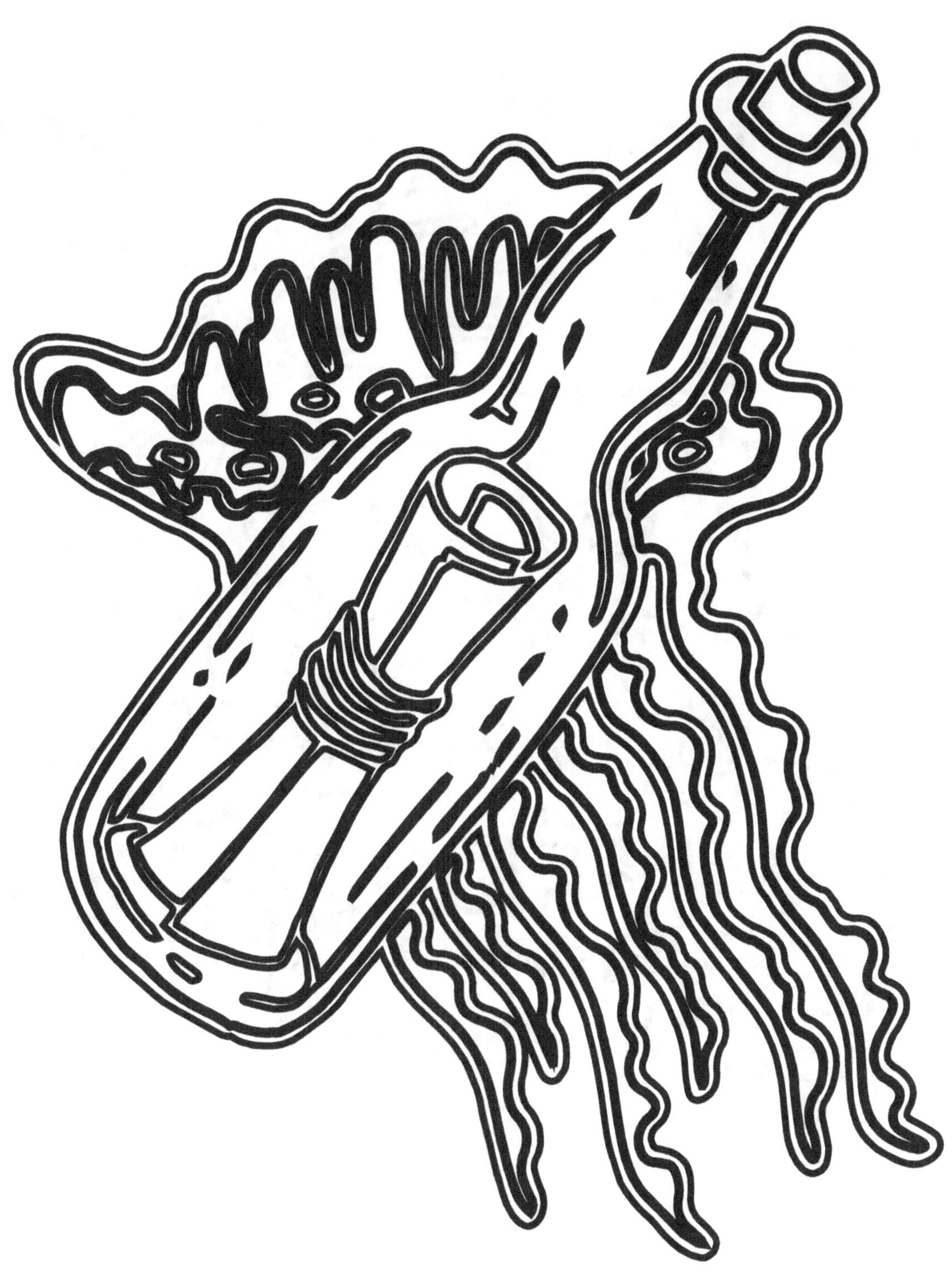

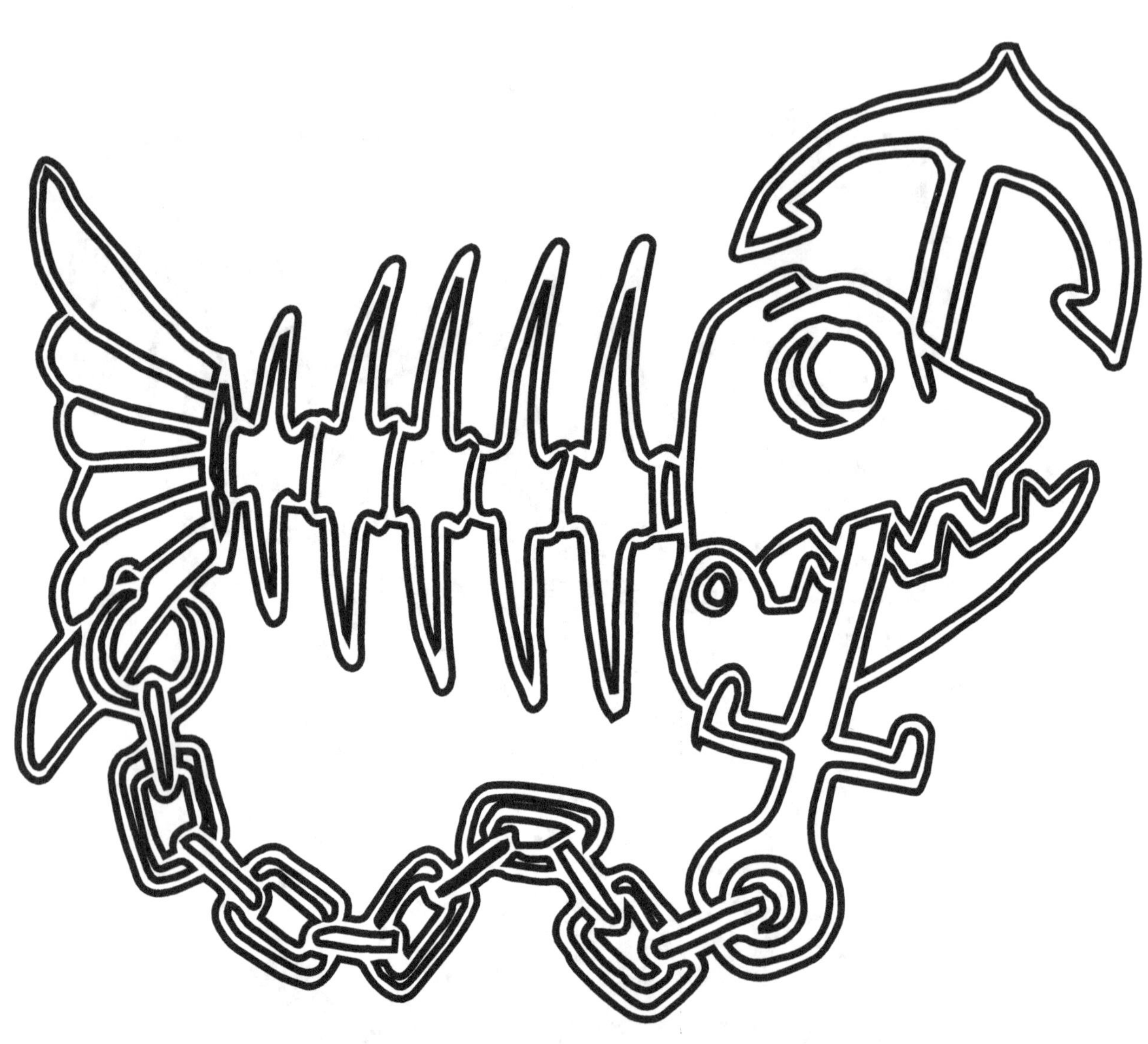

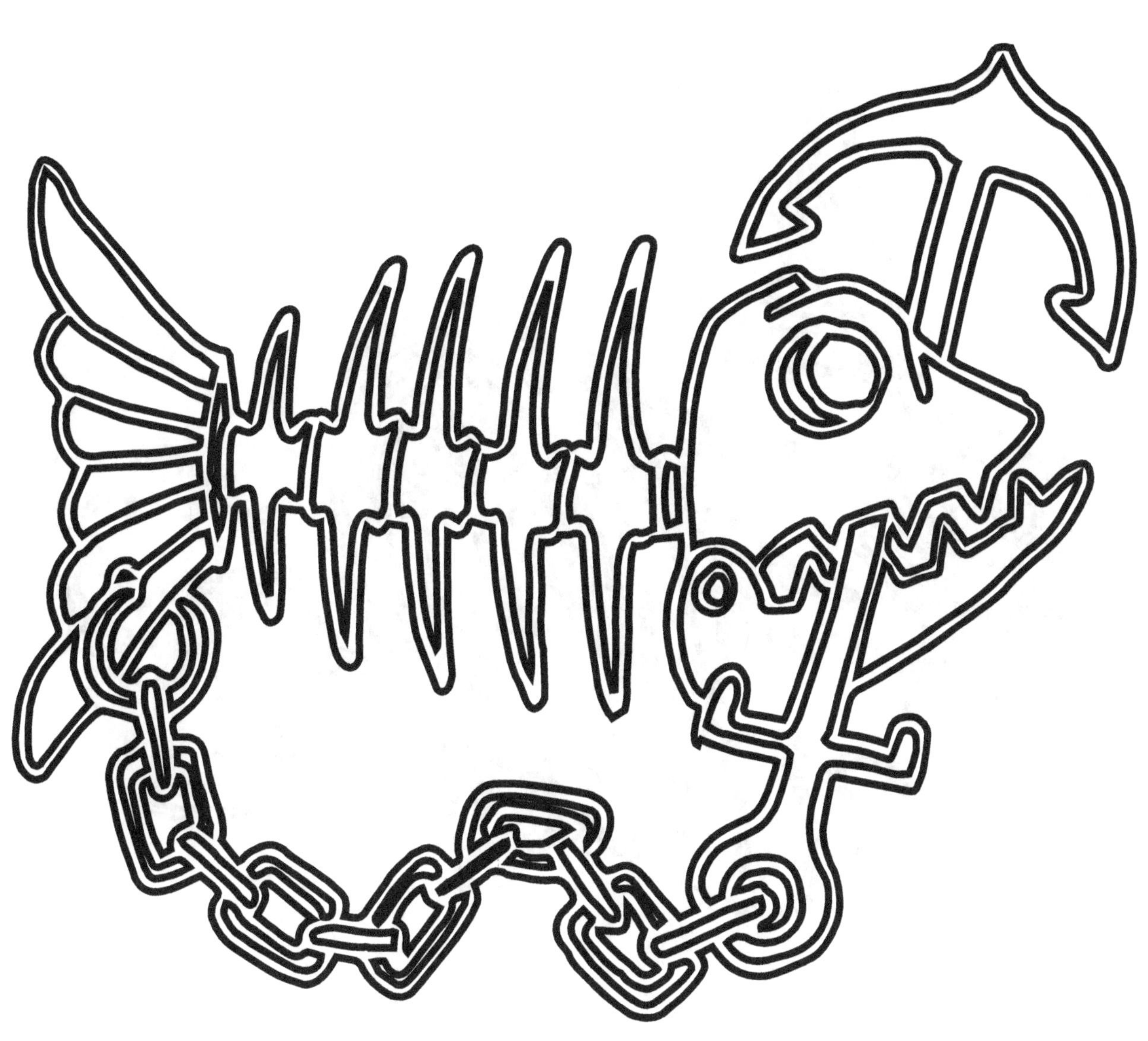

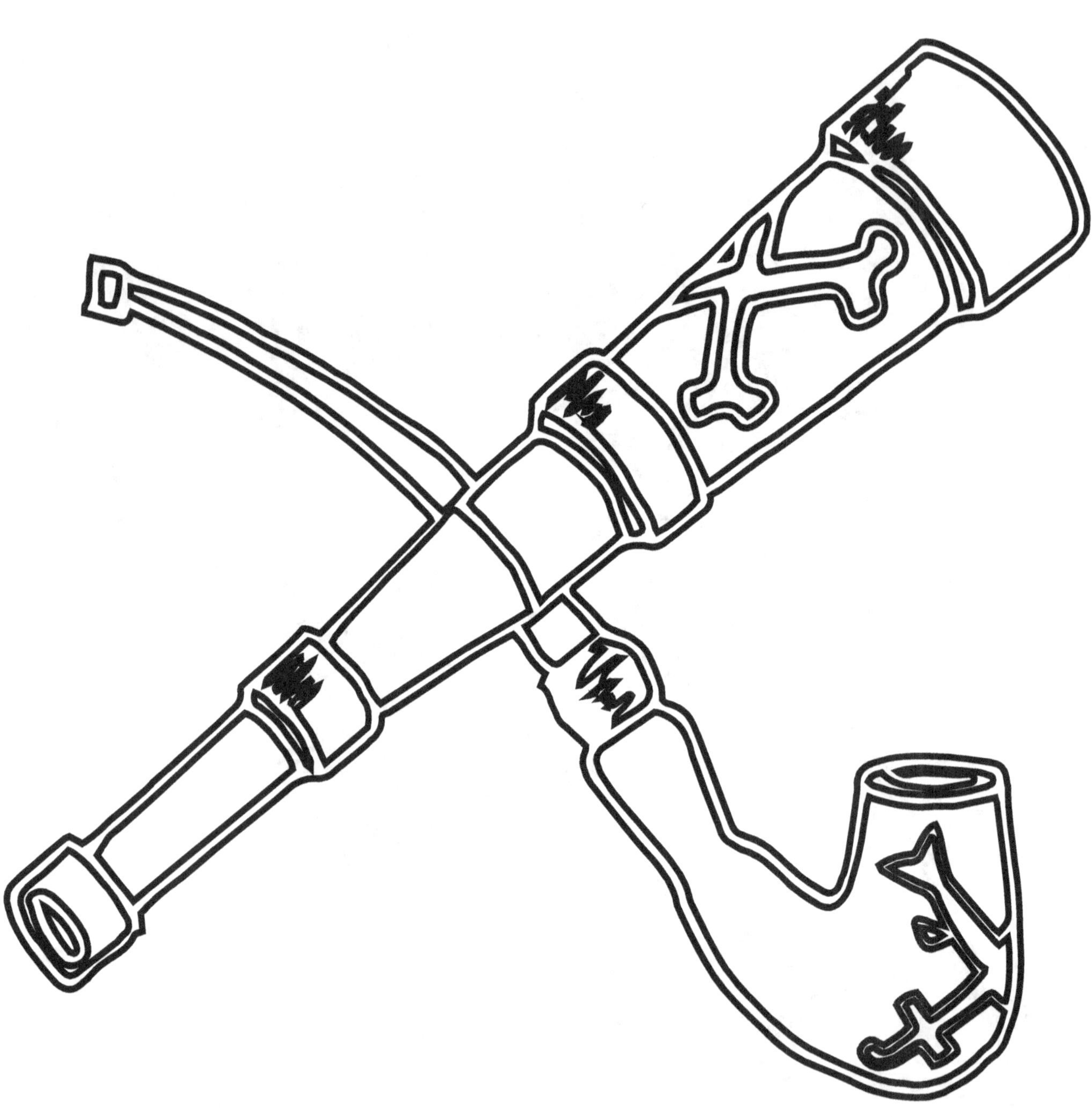

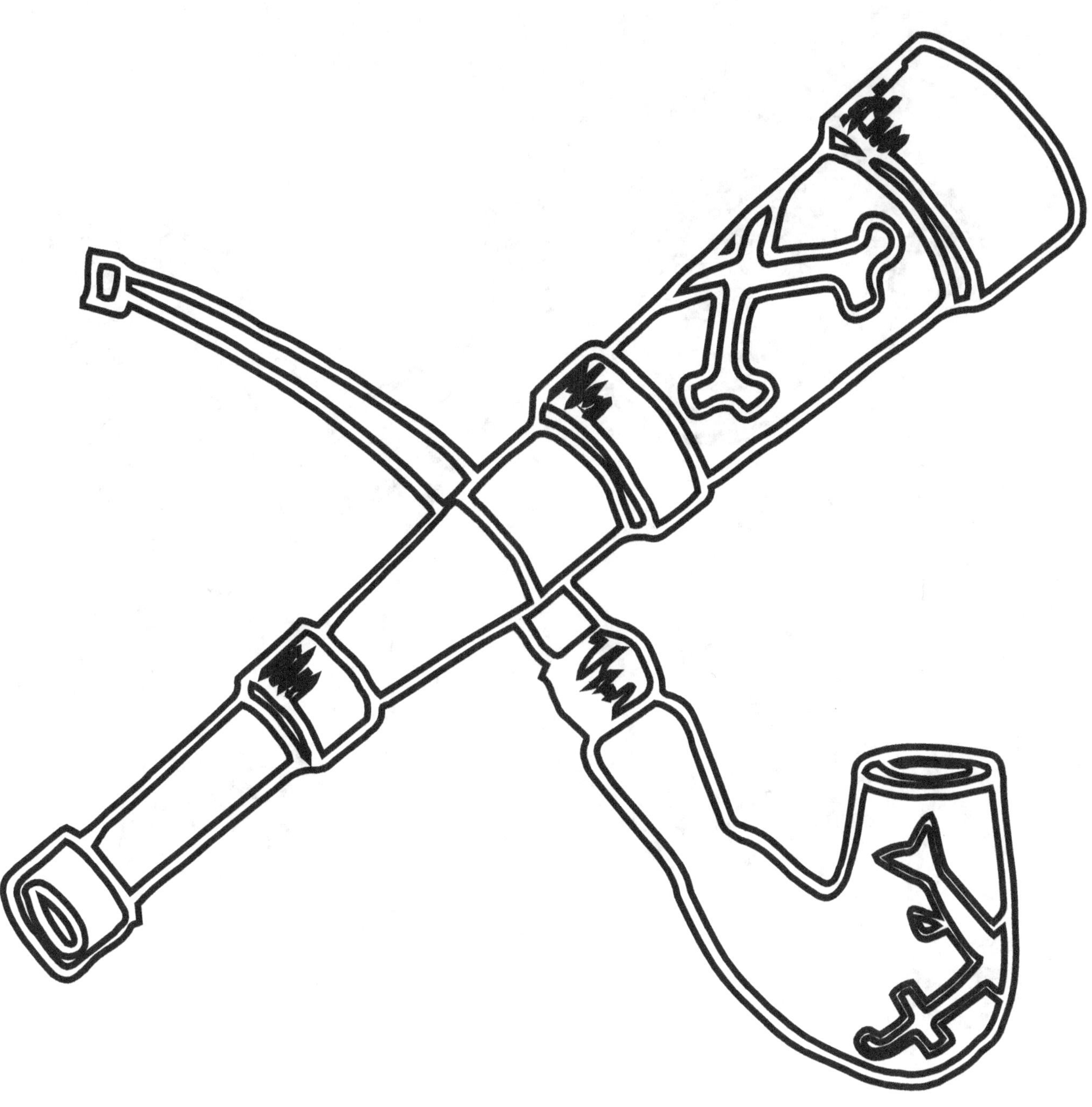